FISH

REPRODUCTION

BookLife
PUBLISHING

©2019
BookLife Publishing Ltd.
King's Lynn
Norfolk PE30 4LS

All rights reserved.
Printed in Malaysia.

A catalogue record for this book is
available from the British Library.

ISBN: 978-1-78637-673-2

Written by:
Joanna Brundle

Edited by:
John Wood

Designed by:
Dan Scase

All facts, statistics, web addresses
and URLs in this book were verified
as valid and accurate at time of
writing. No responsibility for any
changes to external websites or
references can be accepted by
either the author or publisher.

PHOTO CREDITS

All images are courtesy of Shutterstock.com, unless otherwise specified. With thanks to Getty Images, Thinkstock Photo and iStockphoto. Front Cover – Nadzin, panpilai paipa. 2 – panpilai paipa. 4 – Monkey Business Images, Rich Carey, Vlad61. 5 – Lukiyanova Natalia frenta, Christina Siow. 6 – BlueRingMedia, Moushomi. 7 – Andrei Nekrassov, Martin Prochazkacz, dien. 8 – 22August, Mikola Gyorgy. 9 – Ng KW. 10 – Beth Swanson, nounours. 11 – Joao Pedro Silva, Alessandro De Maddalena. 12 – Zacarias Pereira da Mata, SergeUWPhoto. 13 – Rostislav Stefanek, Pranisa Thanatattanon, NERYXCOM. 14 – magnusdeepbelow, Rich Carey. 15 – OneSmallSquare, BlueRingMedia, Designua. 16 – Mike Workman, Andrey Armyagov. 17 – itsnbi, Yann hubert. 18 – Laura Dinraths, Dewald Kirsten. 19 – S.Rohrlach, Steven L. Gordon. 20 – Nicole Griffin Ward, Kristina Vackova. 21 – zaferkizilkaya, Gerald Robert Fischer. 22 – Gleb Tarro, Zykov_Vladimir. 23 – Jarabogu, jack perks. 24 – Raluephoto, DWI YULIANTO. 25 – Toxotes Hun. 26 – Vladimir Wrangel, stockphoto-graf. 27 – Dragon Images, GTS Productions. 28 – Cigdem Sean Cooper, aquapix, Krzysztof Odziomek, Mr. Meijer. 29 – Daniel Huebner, Sergey Uryadnikov. 30 – Daniella Cortis, MP cz. Coral vectors throughout – Baksiabat. Fish vector throughout – Nadzin. Background – Pattern image.

CONTENTS

Words that look like THIS can be found in the glossary on page 31.

WHAT IS REPRODUCTION?

Have you ever wondered how you and all the other animals and plants in our world came to be here? Where did we all come from? These are big questions, but the answer is simple – reproduction. Reproduction is the process by which all living things make more of themselves. It is common to all living things, from the blue whale, the largest animal on Earth, to the tiniest living things that can only be seen under a microscope. Mammals, birds, fish, reptiles, amphibians, insects and plants all need to reproduce. You are here because your parents have reproduced, as their parents did before them.

These grandparents and parents have reproduced to give birth to new GENERATIONS.

THE FIRST FISH-LIKE CREATURES APPEARED ON EARTH AROUND 530 MILLION YEARS AGO.

WHY IS REPRODUCTION IMPORTANT?

Reproduction is important because all living things have a LIFESPAN and will eventually die. They must therefore reproduce to make sure that their SPECIES continues and does not die out. This is sometimes called 'the circle of life'.

School of snapper fish

Do you think we should have some babies?

Let's read on and see how it happens.

SEXUAL AND ASEXUAL REPRODUCTION

Sexual reproduction requires one male and one female parent. New life is made by putting together genetic information (instructions about how growth and development take place) from the two parents. Genetic information is found inside <u>CELLS</u>, including sex cells called gametes. In males, gametes are called sperm. In females, gametes are called eggs. During sexual reproduction, the two gametes join together in a process called fertilisation. When an egg cell and a sperm cell join together, they form a fertilised egg. This then begins to divide over and over again to form an <u>EMBRYO</u>. The embryo grows to become a new lifeform that carries similar genetic information to both parents but is not exactly the same as either.

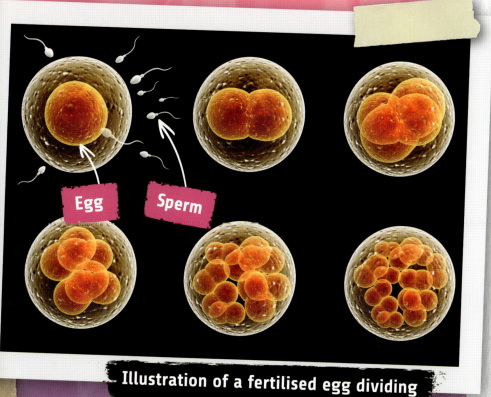

Egg

Sperm

Illustration of a fertilised egg dividing

Asexual reproduction only needs one parent. The young that are produced carry exactly the same genetic information as the parent. Asexual reproduction may take place as a result of a process called parthenogenesis (say: par-thu-no-jen-u-sis), in which eggs develop into embryos without having been fertilised by sperm. Budding, <u>FRAGMENTATION</u> and <u>FISSION</u> are other common forms of asexual reproduction. Asexual reproduction is very rare in animals but is commonly seen in <u>BACTERIA</u>, fungi and plants.

WHEN YOUNG THAT ARE PRODUCED BY ASEXUAL REPRODUCTION HAVE GENETIC INFORMATION WHICH IS EXACTLY THE SAME AS THAT OF THEIR PARENT, THEY ARE CALLED CLONES.

Budding is a form of asexual reproduction in plants. Plantlets grow from the parent plant before detaching and continuing to grow on their own.

Plantlets

So, how do we reproduce?

Well, we're not fungi, bacteria or plants, so I'm guessing that it's probably sexual reproduction for us.

DIFFERENT TYPES OF FISH

The animal kingdom is divided into smaller groups called phyla. Each phylum groups together animals that are alike in important ways. Along with mammals, birds, reptiles and amphibians, fish are vertebrates. This means they have a backbone. Each phylum is then divided into smaller groups called classes. Fish belong to one of three main classes. They are different from other classes of animal because most of them spend their whole lives in water, have fins and breathe through gills. Almost all are cold-blooded. This means that they cannot control their body temperature, which is affected by the temperature of their environment.

Eye

Gills

Dorsal fin

Pectoral fin

Anal fin

Tail

Mouth

NEAR EXTINCTION AND RECOVERY

The walking catfish is unusual because it can survive out of water, breathing OXYGEN in the air and using its spiny front fins to move about.

About 252 million years ago, around nine out of ten fish were wiped out in a MASS EXTINCTION on Earth. They have since recovered and ADAPTED to live in different environments all over the world. They are found in every saltwater HABITAT from the warmest tropical oceans to icy seas. They are also found in all freshwater habitats, from lakes and rivers to swamps and streams.

A SPECIES BECOMES EXTINCT WHEN THERE ARE NO MORE LIVING MEMBERS OF THAT SPECIES.

CLASSES OF FISH

River lamprey

AGNATHANS

Agnathans have no jaws. Their mouths are simply holes in their heads, with horny teeth. They do not usually have scales and they do not have the pairs of fins seen in other classes. Most fish in this class have become extinct, but two groups have survived. These are lampreys and hagfish.

SCIENTISTS THINK THAT THERE ARE CURRENTLY AROUND 34,000 KNOWN LIVING SPECIES OF FISH.

CHONDRICHTHYANS (SAY: CON-DRICK-THEE-ANS)

Fish in this class include sharks, rays and chimaeras such as rat fish. They have paired fins and both an upper and lower jaw, full of teeth. Their skeletons are made of cartilage rather than bone. Cartilage is the same bendy material that makes up our nose and ears. There are over 1,000 species of sharks and rays.

Great white shark

Sharks have rows of teeth, one behind the other. If a tooth is lost, another moves forward to replace it.

OSTEICHTHYANS (SAY: O-STAY-ICK-THEE-ANS)

This group is often called 'bony fish' because they have skeletons made of bone rather than cartilage. Most have bony fins. They also have an operculum. This is a bony flap that covers and protects the gills that fish use to breathe. Common species of bony fish include cod, tuna and salmon, as well as seahorses.

Goldfish are classed as bony fish. They were first kept as pets by the Chinese over a thousand years ago.

COURTSHIP AND MATING

Drummer fish

Male fish display courtship behaviours to attract a female and to warn off other males. Drummer fish make grunting, rumbling sounds to get the female's attention. After building a nest under rocks, the male Lusitanian toadfish makes long, rhythmic whistle-like noises. He is fiercely <u>TERRITORIAL</u> and uses these sounds to defend his chosen nesting site.

Clownfish click their jaws together to scare off other males. Some fish, including groupers, spawn on the day of either a full moon or a new moon, depending on the species. The male grouper tries to impress the female by quivering and showing off the underneath part of his body.

BUILDING SANDCASTLES

Cichlid fish

THE PROCESS OF LAYING EGGS IS CALLED SPAWNING.

Most African cichlid fish live in Lake Malawi, Lake Victoria or Lake Tanganyika in East Africa. Once or twice a year, the males of around 200 species of African cichlids build an underwater bower. This is a sandcastle-shaped structure that will be the nesting site. The male then defends the bower, which he uses to attract a suitable mate. Each species builds a differently shaped sandcastle bower.

MAKING A MASTERPIECE

The Japanese pufferfish creates an underwater masterpiece to get a female's attention. He works non-stop for a week, using only his fins to scoop sand into a complicated pattern. The pattern is a perfectly formed circle. It is made up of ridges, valleys and lines, similar to the sand patterns you may have seen on a beach when the tide has gone out. As he ploughs through the sand, water <u>CURRENTS</u> carry the finest sand particles to the centre of the circle. He even uses shells and pieces of coral or <u>SEDIMENT</u> to decorate his work. If a possible mate approaches, the male stirs up the fine sand at the centre. If the female is impressed, she lays her eggs in the centre. Scientists do not fully understand whether it is the size, shape or pattern that attracts the female. It is hard work building a nest, so a large nest might indicate a strong, fit male partner. The fine sand at the centre of the nest also seems to interest the female.

A Japanese pufferfish has a rather dull appearance but amazing artistic skill.

FEMALE THREE-SPINED STICKLEBACKS CHOOSE A MATE BY DECIDING WHICH MALE HAS THE BRIGHTEST RED BELLY AND WHO DOES THE BEST ZIG-ZAG COURTING 'DANCE'.

Are you going to make me a pretty nest?

Let me think... Sorry, no.

9

OVIPAROUS, VIVIPAROUS AND OVOVIVIPAROUS REPRODUCTION

SEXUAL AND ASEXUAL REPRODUCTION

Bonnethead shark

Nearly all fish reproduce using sexual reproduction. Eggs from the female are fertilised by sperm from the male. A few species, including bonnethead and zebra sharks, have been known to reproduce asexually by means of parthenogenesis (see page 5), but this is very rare.

The female red-bellied piranha lays thousands of eggs in a nest dug by the male.

OVIPAROUS FISH

Most fish are oviparous. This means that they lay eggs in order to reproduce. The female releases her eggs directly into the water. The male then releases his sperm. Females usually release large numbers of small eggs. The eggs are usually fertilised outside the female's body. Fish lay hundreds, thousands or, in some cases, millions of eggs to try to make sure that some survive. Very few survive to hatch from the eggs and, of these, only a few reach adulthood. Fish eggs do not have a shell to protect them from drying out and therefore need to remain in water. The developing embryo is NOURISHED by the yolk. The yolk is contained in a YOLK SAC within the egg. Salmon and trout are examples of oviparous fish.

SEVERAL SPECIES OF SHARK, INCLUDING BAMBOO AND HORN SHARKS, ARE OVIPAROUS, BUT THE EGGS ARE LAID AFTER THEY HAVE BEEN FERTILISED INSIDE THE FEMALE'S BODY (SEE PAGE 11).

VIVIPAROUS FISH

Viviparous fish give birth to live young. The female's eggs are fertilised inside her body and the embryos develop inside her UTERUS. They are attached to and nourished by the mother's body, until they are ready to be born. Several species of shark are viviparous, including the hammerhead, blue and bull species.

OVOVIVIPAROUS FISH

Ovoviviparous fish also give birth to live young. They also produce eggs which are fertilised and develop inside the female, but each embryo is nourished by the yolk in its egg until it is ready to hatch. Some female fish, such as guppies, are able to store sperm inside their bodies and use it to fertilise other eggs later. Most rays, except skates, are ovoviviparous, as are some species of shark, including the great white shark.

Blue-spotted stingray

Young stingray look like tiny adults and are strong swimmers from birth.

GROUPS OF EGGS THAT HATCH OUT AT THE SAME TIME ARE CALLED BROODS.

CLASPERS

Male sharks, rays, skates and chimaeras use body parts called claspers to place their sperm into an opening in the female called her cloaca. They have two claspers, but use only one at a time.

Claspers

Grooves in the claspers act like funnels to direct sperm into the female's cloaca.

FISH EGGS

Most females are able to lay large numbers of eggs at a time because egg-laying requires much less energy than producing live young. For example, the ocean sunfish, also known as the mola, releases over 300 million eggs in a single spawning season. By comparison, great white sharks produce between 2 and 12 live young at a time. Oviparous (egg-laying) fish lay and protect their eggs in one of several ways.

As well as producing more eggs than any other oviparous fish, the ocean sunfish is also one of the world's largest bony fish.

MOUTHBROODERS

A mouthbrooding jawfish carrying its eggs in its mouth

After the eggs have been released and fertilised, mouthbrooders scoop them up and use their mouths to protect the eggs until they hatch. Depending on the species, it may be the male, the female or both parents that look after the eggs in this way. Some, such as the African cichlid female, continue to keep the young in their mouths for a short time after hatching. Mouthbrooders also include cardinal fish, sea catfish and jawfish.

That must make eating a bit tricky.

Mm, I hope we're not mouthbrooders.

NEST BUILDERS

Some fish, such as sticklebacks, build nests made of small sticks or pieces of plant material. Others create bubble nests. The male blows clusters of bubbles on the surface of the water or attached to floating plant material. Once the female has released her eggs beneath the nest, the male quickly picks them up in his mouth and puts them into the bubble nest. He then guards the nest until the eggs hatch. If any fall out, he carefully puts them back inside.

Sticklebacks are found in fresh, salt and BRACKISH water.

Bubble nests protect the eggs and also provide newly hatched young with oxygen and food in the form of MICROORGANISMS attracted to the bubbles.

EGG BURIERS, SCATTERERS AND DEPOSITORS

Rainbow fish are egg depositors.

Egg buriers, such as killifish, bury their eggs in sand or gravel. These species are commonly found in places where the waters dry up at certain times of the year. The fertilised eggs can survive in a DORMANT state until the next rains prompt them to hatch. Egg scatterers, such as goldfish, simply scatter their eggs over a certain area. The male swims through the area and fertilises the eggs by spraying sperm. Egg depositors choose one particular place to lay their eggs, usually on mud, rock or stones.

FISH SPERM ARE CONTAINED IN A MILKY FLUID CALLED MILT.

What do we do?

Let's look at page 24 to find out.

FISH YOUNG

Viviparous and ovoviviparous fish produce a few well-developed young. Being well developed, compared with young hatched from eggs outside the female's body, gives these young a much better chance of survival. Live young are born fully formed and look like tiny copies of their adult parents. Most species of shark reach sexual maturity (the age at which they are ready to reproduce) between 15 and 20 years of age. Some smaller species may take only three to four years.

SHARK YOUNG, KNOWN AS PUPS, ARE BORN WITH A FULL SET OF TEETH.

METAMORPHOSIS

Oviparous fish produce young that go through different stages before becoming adults. This process of change is called metamorphosis. The eggs hatch into larvae which, in turn, grow into tiny, IMMATURE fish called fry. Fry gradually develop into juveniles, sometimes called fingerlings. Juveniles continue to develop to adulthood. At the juvenile stage, they may have different colourings and markings from the adults.

Juvenile emperor angelfish

Juvenile nearing adulthood

Adult

LIFE CYCLE OF OVIPAROUS FISH

Spawning

Some fish, such as Pacific salmon, may spawn only once and then die. Others spawn every year or with a gap of a few years.

Mermaid's purse

Eggs

Eggs carry a yolk sac which is the food supply. Some fish, such as skate, lay their eggs in a protective case, commonly known as a mermaid's purse. A tail and two dark spots that will develop into eyes may be seen inside each egg.

Larvae

Larvae look very different from fry, juveniles and adults. The yolk sac may still be attached to newly hatched larvae. Once the yolk is used up, larvae feed on smaller PLANKTON. Larvae can swim but may drift long distances in currents. Most will not survive.

Fry

Young fish are called fry for the first few months. Fins and scales begin to form.

Juveniles

The young fish are approaching adulthood but are not yet sexually mature (able to reproduce). They have scales and working fins.

Adults

The fish is fully grown and has reached sexual maturity.

FISH PARENTS

Yellow-spotted trigger fish

Most fish are not good parents. Oviparous fish usually take no further care of the eggs after fertilisation. Some species, however, do look after their eggs. They build nests (see page 13) and fiercely defend their nesting sites against predators, including humans. Triggerfish, for example, charge or bite if predators enter their nesting sites. Siamese fighting fish puff out their gills and spread their fins to warn off predators.

FANNING AND CLEANING

Some parents fan the eggs using their fins to keep the water moving. This gives the eggs a good supply of oxygen, which they need to survive. If the water around the eggs becomes **STAGNANT**, the oxygen supply in the water is quickly used up. Some clean the eggs by brushing them with their fins. They use their mouths to remove any diseased or dead eggs. Splash tetra fish leap from the water together, then lay and fertilise their eggs on an overhanging leaf. The male then guards the eggs, splashing them with his tail fin until they are ready to hatch.

Well, you're not very friendly.

At least our eggs will be safe.

Discus fish fan their eggs and keep them clean.

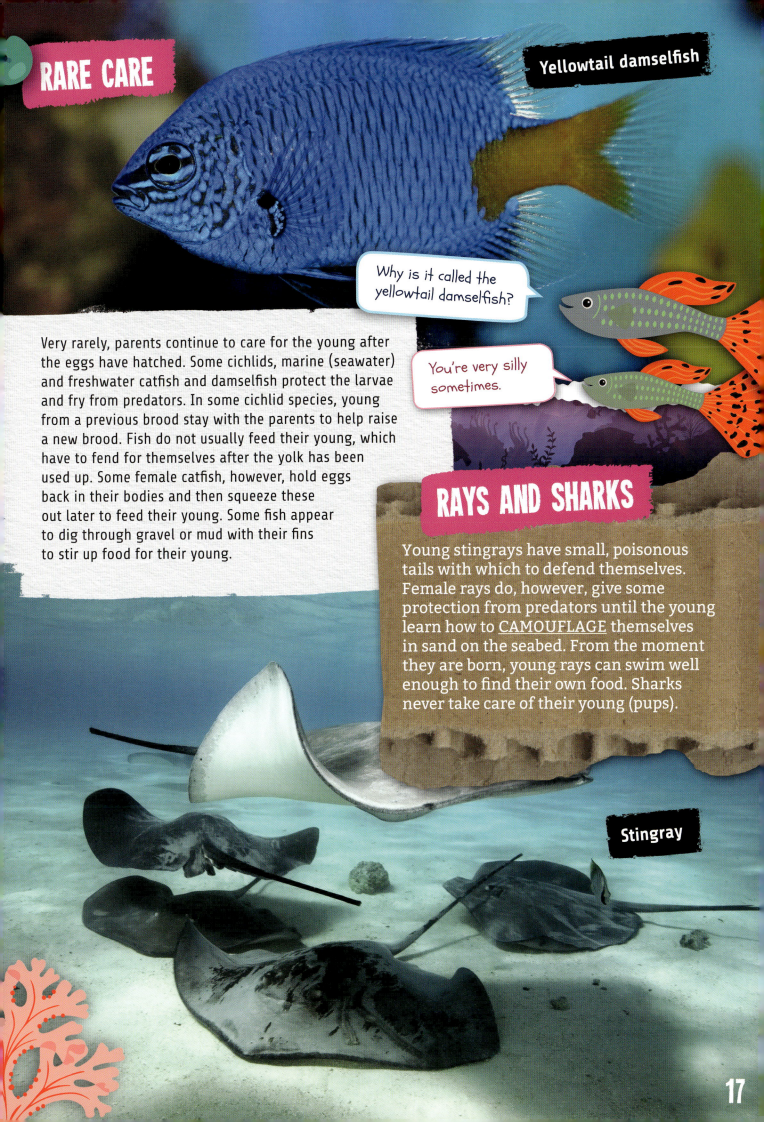

RARE CARE

Yellowtail damselfish

Why is it called the yellowtail damselfish?

You're very silly sometimes.

Very rarely, parents continue to care for the young after the eggs have hatched. Some cichlids, marine (seawater) and freshwater catfish and damselfish protect the larvae and fry from predators. In some cichlid species, young from a previous brood stay with the parents to help raise a new brood. Fish do not usually feed their young, which have to fend for themselves after the yolk has been used up. Some female catfish, however, hold eggs back in their bodies and then squeeze these out later to feed their young. Some fish appear to dig through gravel or mud with their fins to stir up food for their young.

RAYS AND SHARKS

Young stingrays have small, poisonous tails with which to defend themselves. Female rays do, however, give some protection from predators until the young learn how to CAMOUFLAGE themselves in sand on the seabed. From the moment they are born, young rays can swim well enough to find their own food. Sharks never take care of their young (pups).

Stingray

REPRODUCTION IN SEAHORSES

Seahorses belong to a group of fish called Hippocampus. There are thought to be around 45 species of seahorse worldwide. They have a head and neck that look like those of a horse. Their long, curved tails are used to anchor them to sea grasses and corals.

It is easy to see how the seahorse got its name.

SHALL WE DANCE?

Unlike most fish, seahorses usually keep the same partner throughout the breeding season. Sometimes, they mate for life. Each morning, the male and female greet one another. They do this by changing their colours and by swimming side by side and around in circles so that they seem to be dancing. Their tails may be linked together. These displays strengthen their bond with one another until they are ready to mate. At this point, the male begins to show off his brood pouch. This is a pocket on the male's body where the female will place her eggs. He can pump water through the pouch to show the female that the pouch is empty and ready for her eggs.

Do we have to dance?

I hope not. 'Dad dancing' is never a pleasant sight!

The male and female float and spin upwards together. The female then places her unfertilised, pear-shaped eggs into the brood pouch. She uses a special tube-like part, called her ovipositor, to do this. After mating, the male sinks to the bottom and rocks gently from side to side to settle the eggs. The male then releases his sperm into the brood pouch to fertilise the eggs. Amazingly, the male is now pregnant. The embryos take between 10 and 45 days to develop fully, depending on the species and the temperature of the water. They stay in the brood pouch throughout this time, safely tucked away from predators. The pouch provides oxygen and food as well as acting as an <u>INCUBATOR</u>. The time that it takes the embryos to develop is known as the gestation period. The male slowly increases the salinity (saltiness) of the fluid in the pouch. By the time the young are ready to be born, it matches that of the open sea.

The brood pouch of this male White's seahorse is full of developing young.

MALES FIGHT WITH OTHER MALES FOR A FEMALE. THEY LOCK TAILS AND SNAP AT EACH OTHER.

When the young are ready to be born, the male pushes them out of his brood pouch in several spurts. In order to do this, his body produces a series of muscle jerks called contractions. It can be a long process, lasting up to 12 hours. The young are called fry. Some species produce huge numbers of fry, up to 1,500 at a time. These large numbers are important for survival because only one to five out of 1,000 fry will reach adulthood. The others are eaten by predators or may be swept out to sea in currents, away from feeding grounds. The young find other fry that have just been born. They float along in groups, using their tiny tails to hold on to one another and to seagrasses. The young are born fully formed and look exactly like tiny adults. Once released, they never return to the brood pouch.

Newly hatched seahorse fry

Can you see that they are already using their tails to cling to the seagrasses?

Pipefish mother and baby

Pipefish are closely related to seahorses. The male pipefish also has a brood pouch and gives birth to the young.

That's a lot of babies to look after.

Maybe we don't look after ours. Let's look at page 24.

Despite caring for the embryos throughout their development, the male seahorse has no further interest in the fry after they are born. Neither parent gives the fry any care or protection. The young have to look after themselves straight away, finding their own food and hiding from predators. They may spend their first few weeks drifting along amongst plankton near the surface. As they grow, they spend most of their time searching for food. They use their long, thin snouts like vacuum cleaners, sucking their food in and swallowing it whole.

Seahorses are very good at hiding from predators. They camouflage themselves by changing colour.

While the male is pregnant, the female is busy too. She prepares more eggs, ready to place into the brood pouch once it is empty. The male and female begin their greeting and courtship behaviour once again and the male may become pregnant again almost immediately.

Pregnant male Denise pygmy seahorse

This seahorse is one of the smallest species. Adults are only up to about 2.4 centimetres in length and the fry are only about the size of a grain of rice.

REPRODUCTION IN SALMON

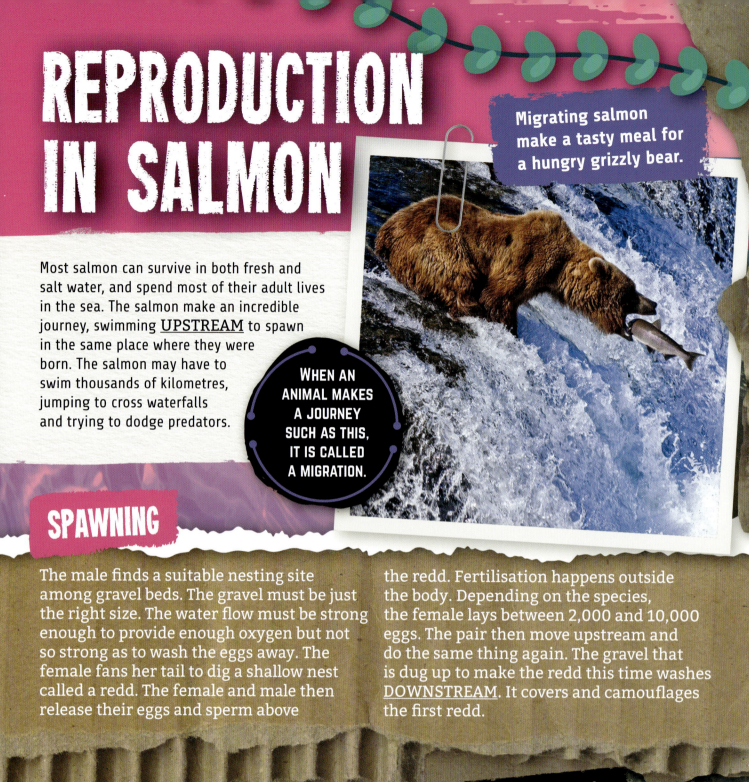

Migrating salmon make a tasty meal for a hungry grizzly bear.

Most salmon can survive in both fresh and salt water, and spend most of their adult lives in the sea. The salmon make an incredible journey, swimming UPSTREAM to spawn in the same place where they were born. The salmon may have to swim thousands of kilometres, jumping to cross waterfalls and trying to dodge predators.

WHEN AN ANIMAL MAKES A JOURNEY SUCH AS THIS, IT IS CALLED A MIGRATION.

SPAWNING

The male finds a suitable nesting site among gravel beds. The gravel must be just the right size. The water flow must be strong enough to provide enough oxygen but not so strong as to wash the eggs away. The female fans her tail to dig a shallow nest called a redd. The female and male then release their eggs and sperm above the redd. Fertilisation happens outside the body. Depending on the species, the female lays between 2,000 and 10,000 eggs. The pair then move upstream and do the same thing again. The gravel that is dug up to make the redd this time washes DOWNSTREAM. It covers and camouflages the first redd.

Salmon eggs hatching

Salmon eggs are orange and about the size of a pea.

Baby salmon, called alevins, hatch after three to four months. At first, they feed on their yolk sac. They grow to become fry and then parr. After about a year, they migrate downstream to the sea. At this stage, they are known as smolt. Before entering the sea, they spend time in brackish water at the mouth of the river, getting used to life in salt water. Smolt live together in groups close to the shore. As adults, they swim farther out to sea. After two to five years, depending on their species, the adult salmon are ready to reproduce. They adjust to fresh water in the river mouth and then begin their incredible journey upstream returning to their place of birth to spawn.

Salmon parr have markings that look like fingerprints on their sides.

Adult salmon have silver-blue scales with black spots.

Salmon are very clever, aren't they?

Are we that smart?

Er, no.

FINDING THEIR WAY

Scientists think that salmon use the Earth's magnetic field as a compass. They seem to remember the magnetic field at the place where they enter the sea and to find it again when they return to spawn. They then appear to use remembered smells to find their particular stream.

REPRODUCTION IN SIAMESE FIGHTING FISH

Siamese fighting fish are a small, colourful species. In the wild, they are found in shallow waters across Asia, but they are also commonly kept as pets because of their beautiful appearance. They originally came from Thailand. Thailand used to be known as Siam, which gave the fish their name. Males fight aggressively with other males. These fish are also known as bettas, named after the ancient Asian Bettah tribe, who were fierce warriors.

Siamese fighting fish display bright colours and flowing fins.

NEST-BUILDING AND SPAWNING

When the male is ready to mate, he builds a bubble nest. The bubbles are coated with <u>SALIVA</u>, which helps them to stick to one another. The nest provides a moist, clean environment, with plenty of oxygen. When the female is ready to spawn, she develops a striped pattern on her body. An egg spot can be seen, which is the place where her eggs will be released. The male may flare his fins and the female may flare back. After he has made the nest, the male fish waits underneath it for a female partner to mate with.

So, I'm really rather beautiful.

Actually, we males are more colourful and we have longer fins.

Male blowing a bubble nest

FERTILISATION AND BROODING

As soon as the female releases her eggs, the male releases milt to fertilise them. He picks the eggs up in his mouth and places them in the nest. He then guards the nest, making repairs and returning any eggs that fall out. Once she has laid her eggs, the female leaves. The male may chase her away as she might try to eat the eggs. The eggs hatch after three days, but the young usually stay in the protection of the bubble nest for a short time.

Male collecting eggs that have fallen from the nest

THE LABYRINTH <u>ORGAN</u> IS IMPORTANT FOR SURVIVAL BECAUSE, IN THE SHALLOW WATERS OF THEIR NATURAL HABITATS, THERE MIGHT NOT BE MUCH OXYGEN.

TWO WAYS TO BREATHE

I think we should get started.

Agreed! Start blowing bubbles please.

After they have used up the yolk, the young move away from the safety of the nest and begin life alone. Neither parent provides any further care. The young continue to develop, breathing oxygen from the water through their gills. After a few weeks, they also develop a lung-like organ, called the labyrinth organ. This allows them to breathe oxygen from the air at the surface through their mouths. They reach sexual maturity after about three months.

FISH UNDER THREAT

Worldwide, over 1,400 species of fish are at risk of extinction. Pollution and loss of habitat are partly to blame, but the main problem is overfishing. Bottom trawling involves dragging netting along the seabed.

Gill nets are like fences on the seabed. If fish try to swim out of them, they are caught by their gills. Both of these types of fishing catch juvenile fish that have not yet reproduced.

Beluga sturgeon take up to 25 years to reach sexual maturity. They are endangered (at risk of being wiped out) due to overfishing with gill nets.

CORAL REEFS

Around a third of the world's sea fish species live on coral reefs. Problems caused by humans, such as GLOBAL WARMING and pollution, threaten about three-quarters of the world's coral reefs, where fish feed and reproduce.

Coral reefs provide food, shelter and safe places to spawn.

SHARKS

You might think that sharks are a greater threat to humans than the other way around. In fact, because sharks reproduce slowly and have few young, they are greatly at risk from dangers caused by humans. These include plastic pollution and overfishing for their meat and fins. Some, such as daggernose and angel sharks, are CRITICALLY ENDANGERED.

SEAHORSES

Seahorses are under threat worldwide. They are used in traditional Chinese medicines. International trade in these medicines is thought to result in around 150 million seahorses being taken from the oceans every year. Seahorses are also dried and sold as souvenirs. An estimated 1 million are sold each year as pets, most of which die soon afterwards.

Undersea explorer Jacques Cousteau (1910–1997) studied the effects of pollution on marine creatures. The Cousteau Society, founded in 1973, continues to teach people about marine conservation.

CONSERVATION

Fishing is an important food source and employs more than 35 million people worldwide. Charities, such as Greenpeace and organisations such as the Marine Stewardship Council (MSC), are involved. They are working to try to find ways to make fishing SUSTAINABLE, whilst protecting food supplies and jobs. Sir David Attenborough is a naturalist and television presenter. His programmes have educated people about issues such as plastic pollution and the effect it has on reproduction in all marine animals.

WHAT CAN YOU DO TO HELP?

You can help by making sure that your family buys sustainable fish. Recycling and re-using plastic materials will help to create less pollution. Try to get involved with conservation charities such as the WWF (Worldwide Fund for Nature).

FASCINATING FISHY FACTS

Pygmy goby

Fish with short lifespans reach sexual maturity more quickly than those with longer lifespans. A tiny coral reef fish called the sign eviota, or pygmy goby, lives its whole life cycle in eight weeks, reaching adulthood within five weeks.

Juvenile zebra shark

Adult zebra sharks don't look like zebras at all – they have spots. It is the pups that have black and white stripes. The stripes warn off predators and make the pups look like poisonous sea snakes. The pups even swim like sea snakes.

Adult zebra shark

Most species have separate males and females, but some species are hermaphrodites. This means that they have both testes (the organs that produce sperm) and ovaries (the organs that produce eggs). As they only produce either eggs or sperm at a time, however, the eggs must be fertilised by sperm from another fish. Some hermaphrodite fish species begin life as one sex and switch to the other later in life.

Clownfish begin life as males but switch to females later.

Do you think fish can fly? It's true – there are around 40 species of flying fish. When they are threatened by predators such as tuna and swordfish, they can launch themselves up and out of the water. They do this by beating their tails very fast. They spread their pectoral fins and use them like wings to glide through the air. Flying fish mate in the open ocean where currents are weak. The female spawns her eggs near the surface of the water. Sticky threads glue the eggs to seaweed or other floating plant material. Newly hatched young have whiskers that make them look like plants and camouflage them from predators.

Flying fish can glide for up to 400 metres.

Mobula rays are also known as flying rays. They launch themselves at speed head first, up and out of the water. They land, however, with a loud splash as they belly-flop back into the water. Scientists think that these belly-flops may be part of their courtship behaviour, as well as a way of 'talking' to one another.

Mobula rays jumping

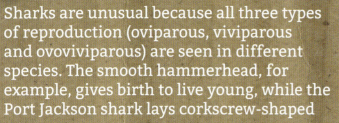

Sharks are unusual because all three types of reproduction (oviparous, viviparous and ovoviviparous) are seen in different species. The smooth hammerhead, for example, gives birth to live young, while the Port Jackson shark lays corkscrew-shaped egg cases. The grey nurse shark gives birth to live pups that hatch from eggs inside her. The gestation period differs between different species. Basking sharks may be pregnant for three years.

The corkscrew shape of Port Jackson egg cases means that they can be firmly wedged into rock <u>CREVICES</u>. Their colour camouflages them by making them look like seaweed.

Sand tiger shark

Among some sharks, such as the sand tiger, there is a struggle for survival even before the young are born. While still in the uterus, the one or two largest embryos kill and eat the others. The surviving pups are born well developed and already up to a metre in length. That's one-third of the length of an adult.

Some fish, such as the Pacific white skate, lay their eggs close to hydrothermal vents. These are openings in the sea bed where water that has been warmed by boiling, liquid rock under the Earth's surface spews out. The vents provide warmth for the developing young.

HYDRO MEANS 'TO DO WITH WATER'. THERMAL MEANS 'TO DO WITH HEAT'.

GLOSSARY

ADAPTED changed over time to suit different conditions

BACTERIA tiny, single-called organisms

BRACKISH fresh water and salt water mixed together

CAMOUFLAGE a way of hiding something so that it looks like its surroundings

CELLS the basic units that make up all living things

CREVICES narrow gaps in rock

CRITICALLY ENDANGERED threatened to the point of becoming almost extinct

CURRENTS continuous movements of a body of water in a particular direction

DORMANT temporarily inactive but able to become active again

DOWNSTREAM in the direction of the mouth of a river

EMBRYO an unborn or unhatched young in the process of development

FISSION a form of asexual reproduction in which the parent cells of an organism divide to make new cells that are exactly the same as the parent cells

FRAGMENTATION a form of asexual reproduction in which an organism splits into fragments, each of which becomes a new individual that is exactly the same as the parent

GENERATIONS groups of animals of the same species that are roughly the same age

GLOBAL WARMING the gradual rise in the Earth's temperature

HABITAT the natural environment in which animals or plants live

IMMATURE not yet fully grown or developed

INCUBATOR a warm box, designed to keep young at the best temperature for their growth and development

LIFESPAN the period of time for which a person, animal or plant lives or is expected to live

MASS EXTINCTION the wiping out, to the point where none remain, of a large number of species

MICROORGANISMS simple lifeforms that include bacteria, algae and fungi

NOURISHED supplied with food and everything needed for healthy development

ORGAN a part of the body, such as the heart or liver, that has a particular function

OXYGEN a colourless gas found in air and dissolved in water that all life needs

PLANKTON tiny living creatures that float and drift in seas and rivers and play an important part in the food chain

SALIVA watery fluid released by glands in the mouth

SEDIMENT small pieces of solid materials such as rock that settle at the bottom of water

SPECIES a group of very similar animals or plants that can produce young together

STAGNANT not flowing or running

SUSTAINABLE able to be used without damaging future generations

TERRITORIAL defending an area against enemies or intruders

UPSTREAM against the flow of the current, towards the source of a river

UTERUS an organ inside the female body for containing and nourishing young before they are born

YOLK SAC a membrane, or thin layer in an egg, that encloses the yolk

INDEX